Andy's Handy-Dandy Bubble-Band-Beanie

by Sarah Weeks

Illustrated by Albert Lemant

MODERN CURRICULUM PRESS

Pearson Learning Group

"Here it is! My best invention yet," cried Andy as he ran into the kitchen. Mary, his wife, was reading the newspaper. She smiled. She was used to Andy's showing her his inventions. He was always making something in his lab.

Mary looked up. "What do you call it, dear?" she asked.

"Andy's Handy-Dandy Bread Warmer!" said Andy proudly. "Here is how to make it work. First plug it in. Next put in a slice of bread. Then push the button. Wait a bit. Then your warm bread will pop up!"

"You have great ideas, dear, but someone has already invented the Bread Warmer," said Mary. "People call it a toaster."

"Really?" said Andy.

"Yes," said Mary as she patted his arm. "Don't worry, I'm sure you will come up with another invention."

Andy nodded.

"Another invention," said Andy as he picked up the Handy-Dandy Bread Warmer. He headed back to his lab to start on a new invention.

"Good luck, dear," called Mary.

"Thank you," said Andy as he closed the door behind him. "I will need it."

A few hours later, Mary heard a strange sound coming from Andy's lab. Suddenly, Andy threw open the door. He ran into the room pulling his new invention behind him. He was very excited. His glasses had slipped down his nose. His notes were flying everywhere.

"What is that?" asked Mary.

"For your information, my dear, this is something that no one should ever be without."

"What is it called?" asked Mary.

"I call it Andy's Handy-Dandy Dirt Sucker."

Mary looked at the odd invention. She did not say anything about the black smoke that came out of it.

"You have great ideas, Andy, but someone has already invented the Dirt Sucker too," said Mary. "People call it a vacuum cleaner."

"Really?" said Andy.

"Yes," said Mary, as she patted his arm.

Andy nodded.

"Thanks for the information," said Andy as he picked up his Handy-Dandy Dirt Sucker and went back to the lab.

"Good luck, dear," called Mary.

"Thank you," said Andy as he closed the door behind him. "I'm going to need it."

Andy stayed in his lab for a long time. Finally he came out.

"Do you have another invention to show me, dear?" asked Mary. She looked to see if he had anything in his hands. But there was nothing.

"Don't you have anything new to show me?" asked Mary.

"No, I don't," said Andy sadly. "I tried to think of something new. I thought hard. But everything I came up with was something someone else had already thought of. Do you have any suggestions? If not, I think I will just go for a walk."

Mary watched as Andy went to get his hat.

"What is that amazing thing on your head?" asked Mary, pointing to the strange-looking thing sitting on top of Andy's head.

"This?" said Andy, putting his hand up to his head.

"Yes, that," said Mary. She could not take her eyes off Andy's head.

"This is my hat," said Andy.

"I have never seen anything quite like it," said Mary.

"Really? Do you like it?" asked Andy.

"Yes, I do," said Mary. "Where did it come from?"

"I invented it," said Andy. "It keeps my head warm. And, for your information, it also plays music and blows bubbles."

"Show me how to make it work," said Mary.

"Sure," said Andy.

"This is by far the best invention you have ever made," said Mary as she and Andy danced round and round in the bubbles.

"Do you think so?" said Andy.

"Yes, but it needs a name," said Mary.

"Hmm," said Andy.

"How about, Andy's Handy-Dandy Bubble-Band Beanie?" suggested Mary.

"Perfect," said Andy with a smile.

So Andy and Mary danced happily in the bubbles, as the Handy-Dandy Bubble-Band Beanie played on and on.